Jazz Standards FOR PIANO

ARRANGED BY TOM COPPOLA

T0058965

ISBN 978-0-7935-8671-4

First printing 1997; This printing 2019

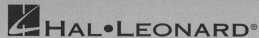

HAL•LEONARD®

7777 W. BLUEMOUND RD. P.O. BOX 13819 MILWAUKEE, WI 53213

Visit Hal Leonard Online at
www.halleonard.com

JAZZ STANDARDS FOR PIANO

This book is dedicated to Antonio Cantuaria Guimaraes, former Ambassador to the United States from Brazil, whose enthusiasm and support were invaluable. My intent was to harmonize standards and jazz tunes the way professionals do, with all the upper tensions of the chords presented in a logical and comprehensible way. The general effect is to sound very sophisticated, while playing material which is accessible and easy to play.

There are several tunes associated with Bill Evans, and these are rendered in voicings and a style reminiscent of Bill. Likewise, "Lush Life" is marked, "...Powell or Tatum in a ballad mode...," and "April in Paris," "...a Basie groove." It is important to refer to recordings. Some tunes are marked with several tempo suggestions. Some are marked, "try different syncopations." All can be considered frameworks for more elaborate improvisation. The reader is also encouraged to try a similar approach on new tunes.

Tom Coppola

ABOUT THE ARRANGER

Pianist Tom Coppola has toured with Herbie Mann, Peggy Lee, and Marvin Gaye. He has recorded with Herbie Mann (*Fire Island*, Atlantic SD 19112), Chic (*CHIC*, Atlantic SD 19153 – platinum), Lenny White (*Attitude*, Elektra 60232), and Paul Simon (*Hearts and Bones*, Warner Bros. 23942 – gold). Tom wrote, arranged, and produced prerecorded music for NBC's *Saturday Night Live* from 1984–1990. In 1994, he received his Master's in Jazz Studies from the University of Southern California, studying with Shelley Berg. He minored in film scoring, studying with Buddy Baker. He is a former adjunct professor of jazz studies at University of North Carolina at Asheville, and Mars Hill University, North Carolina.

Contact: thomascoppola@verizon.net
Website: tomcoppolajazz.com

BUT BEAUTIFUL

Words by JOHNNY BURKE
Music by JIMMY VAN HEUSEN

ALICE IN WONDERLAND
from Walt Disney's ALICE IN WONDERLAND

Words by BOB HILLIARD
Music by SAMMY FAIN

APRIL IN PARIS

A Basie groove. (advanced)

Words by E.Y. HARBURG
Music by VERNON DUKE

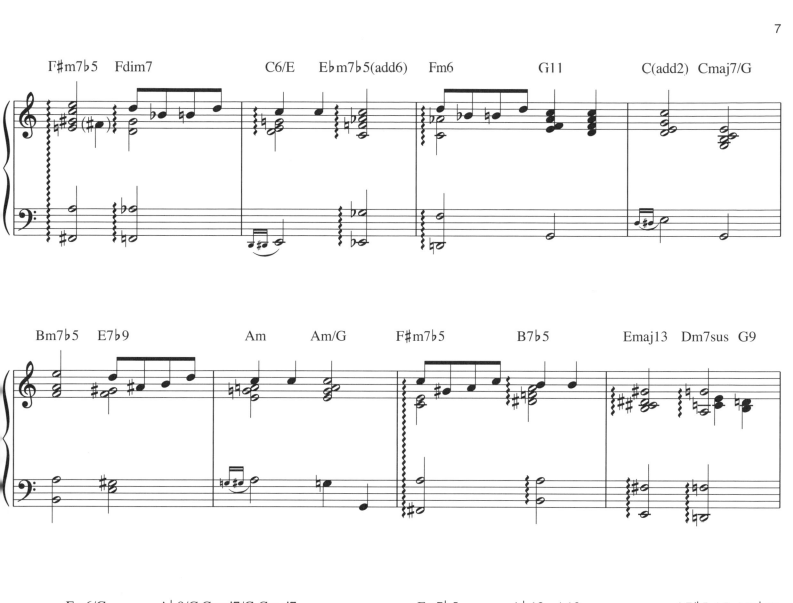

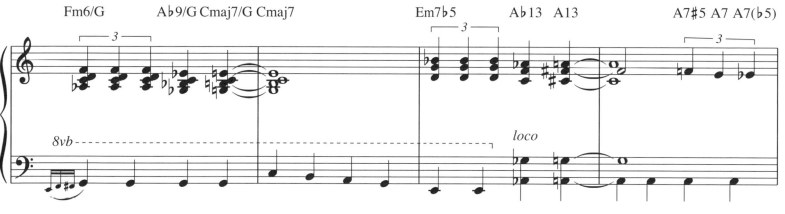

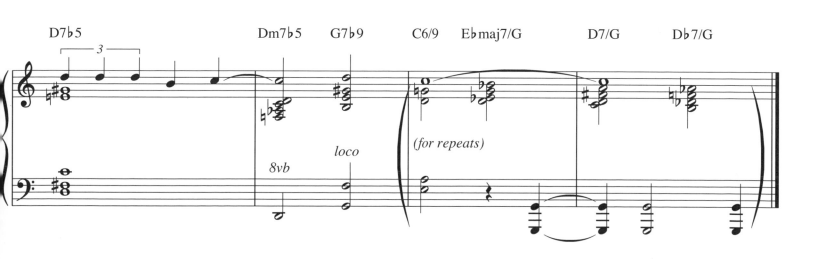

AUTUMN LEAVES
(Les Feuilles Mortes)

Experiment with varying the tempo and rhythms.
In the style of Bill Evans.

English lyric by JOHNNY MERCER
French lyric by JACQUES PREVERT
Music by JOSEPH KOSMA

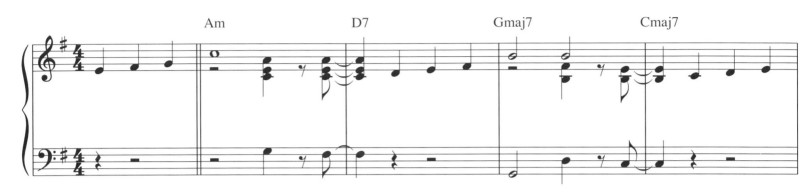

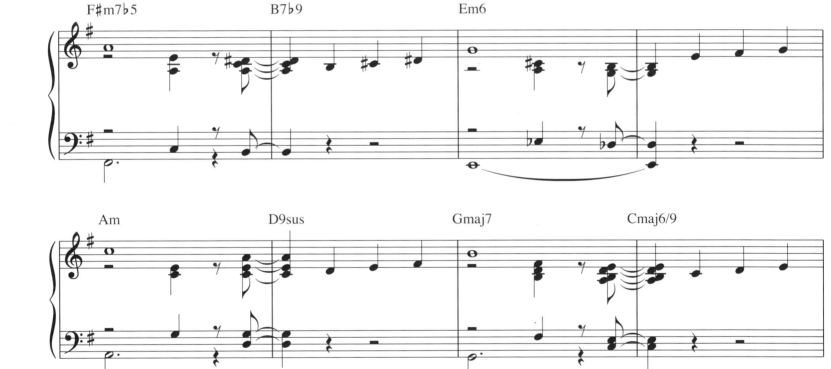

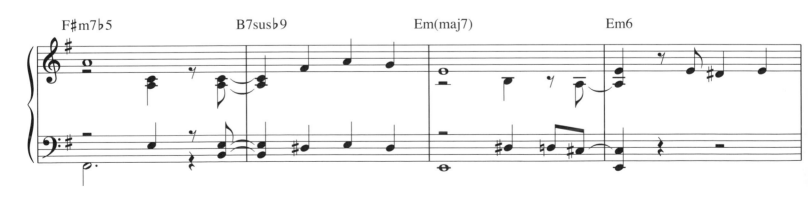

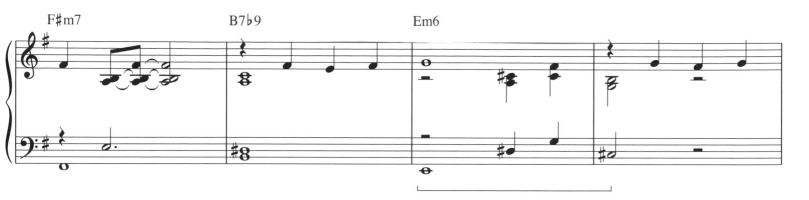

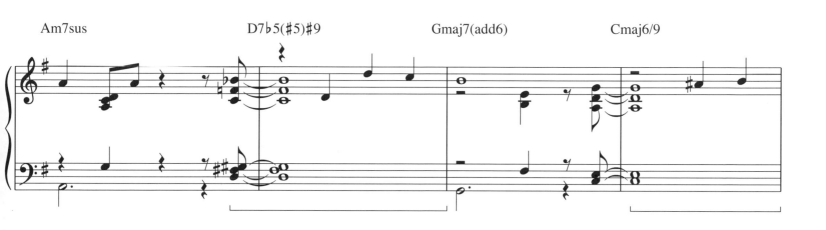

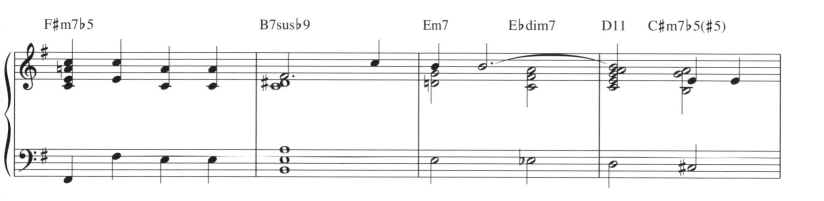

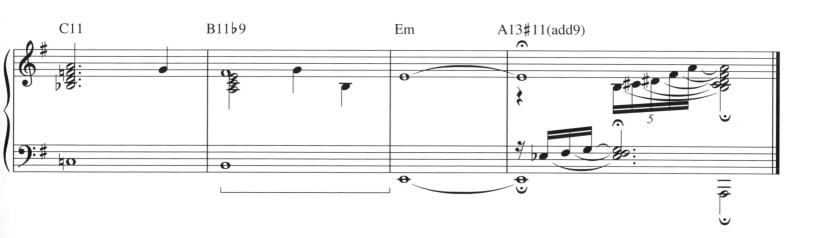

EVERYTHING HAPPENS TO ME

Words by TOM ADAIR
Music by MATT DENNIS

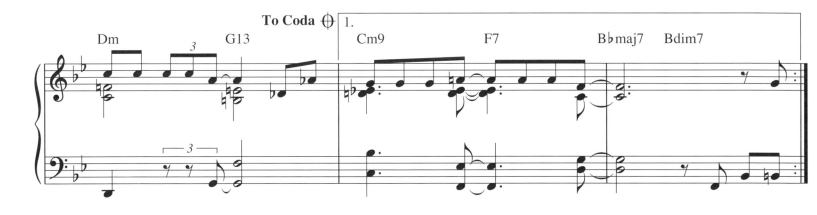

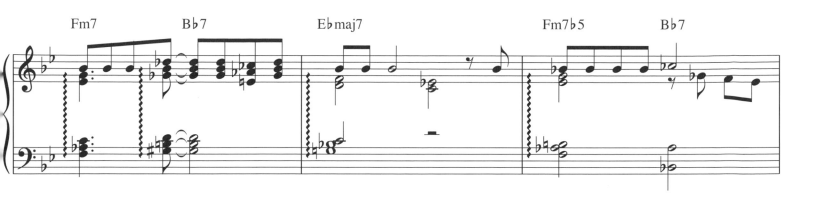

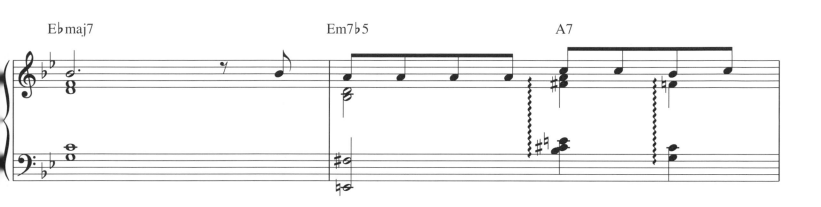

D.S. al Coda

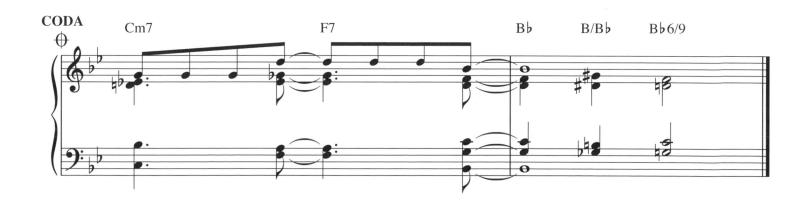

GIRL TALK
from the Paramount Picture HARLOW

Words by BOBBY TROUP
Music by NEAL HEFTI

* This last chord of bar 10, the third of a triplet, is anticipated for the one of bar 11.
One may repeat this process to good effect before one of bar two, three of bar 3,
one of bar 5, one of bar 8, etc.

I'M ALL SMILES

from THE YEARLING

Dedicated to Bill Evans.

Lyric by HERBERT MARTIN
Music by MICHAEL LEONARD

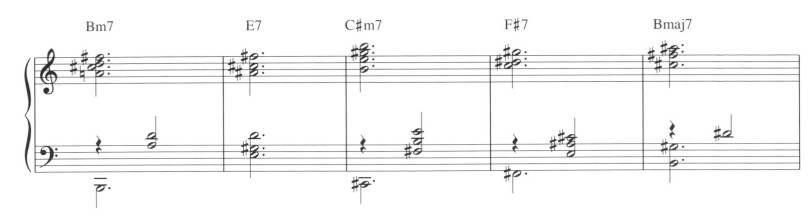

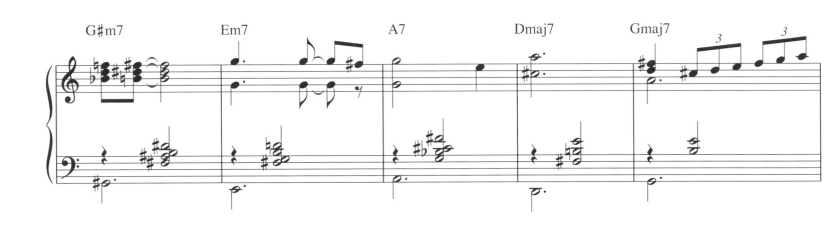

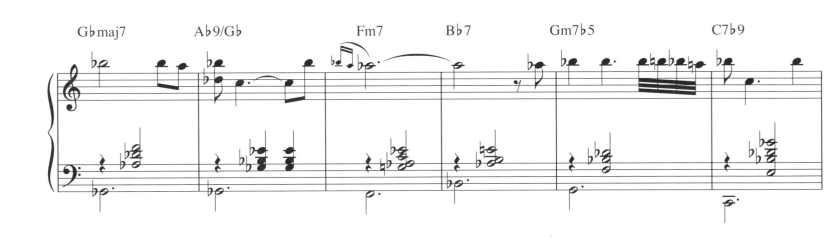

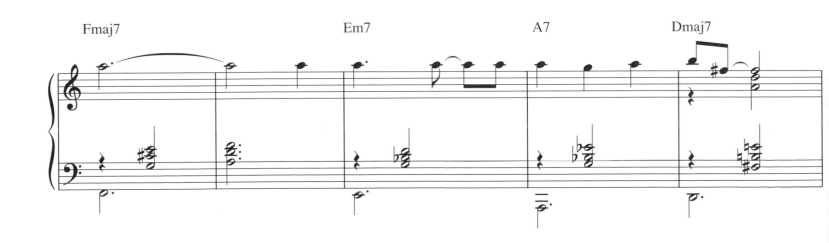

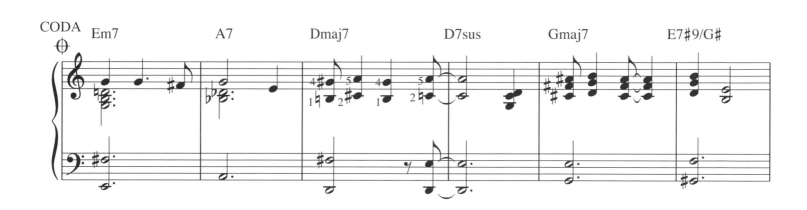

HOW HIGH THE MOON

from TWO FOR THE SHOW

Try syncopating quarter notes variously.

Words by NANCY HAMILTON
Music by MORGAN LEWIS

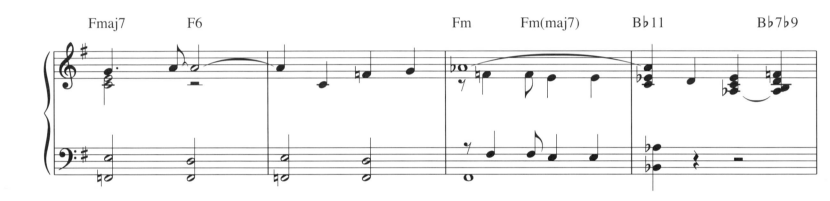

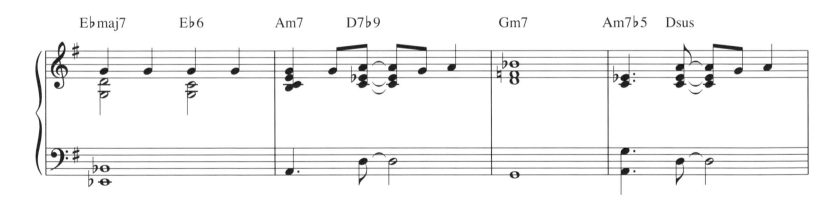

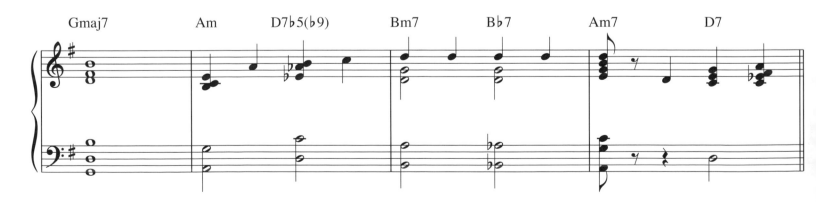

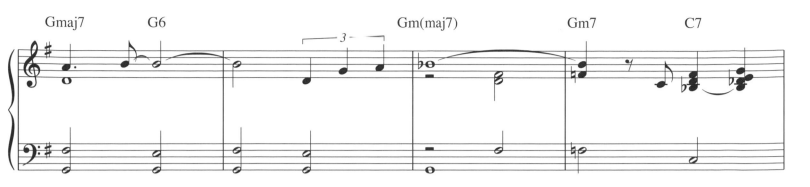

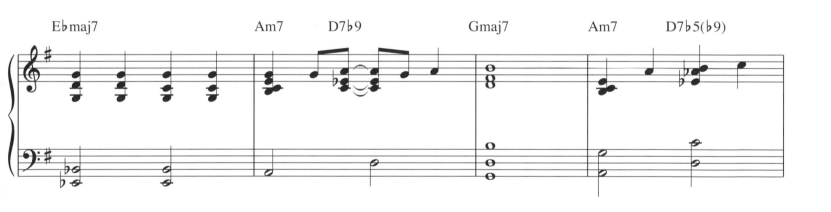

optional rhythm

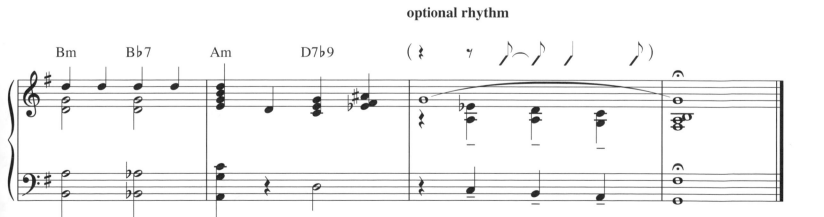

I DIDN'T KNOW WHAT TIME IT WAS

from TOO MANY GIRLS

Words by LORENZ HART
Music by RICHARD RODGERS

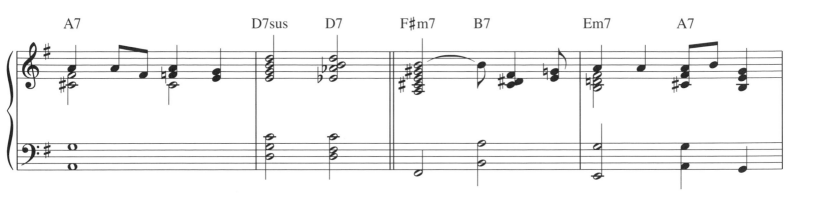

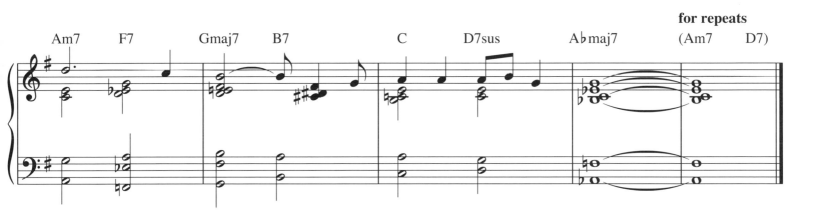

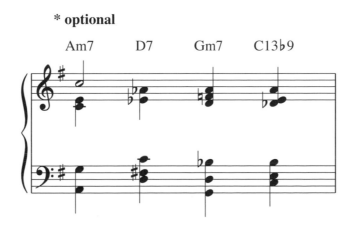

I'LL REMEMBER APRIL

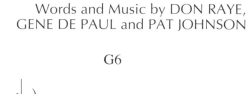

Words and Music by DON RAYE,
GENE DE PAUL and PAT JOHNSON

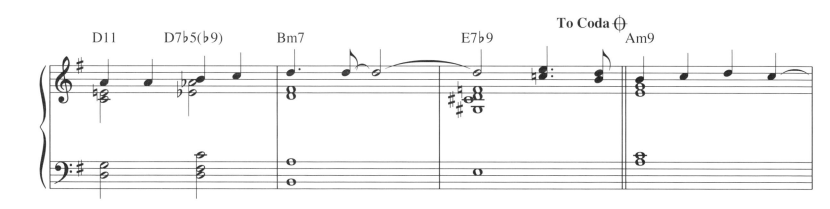

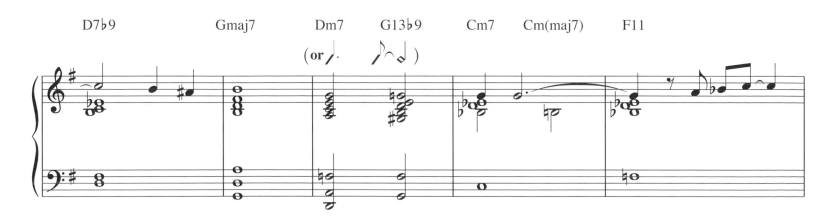

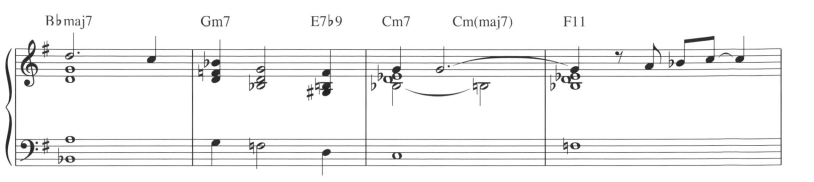

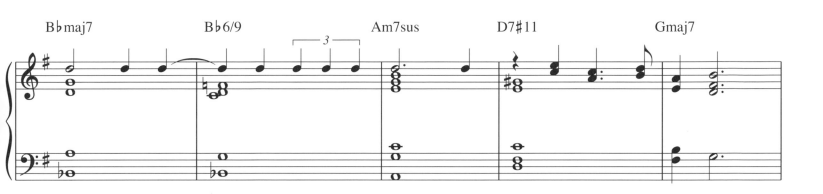

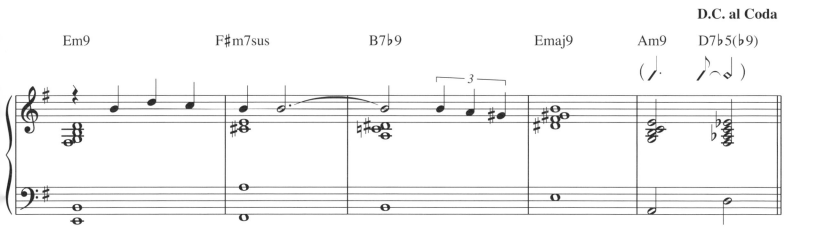

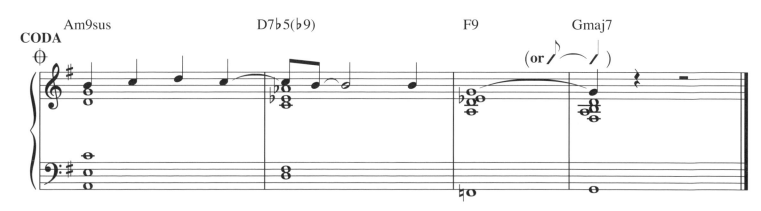

Continue syncopations, simile, where appropriate.

THE NEARNESS OF YOU

from the Paramount Picture ROMANCE IN THE DARK

Words by NED WASHINGTON
Music by HOAGY CARMICHAEL

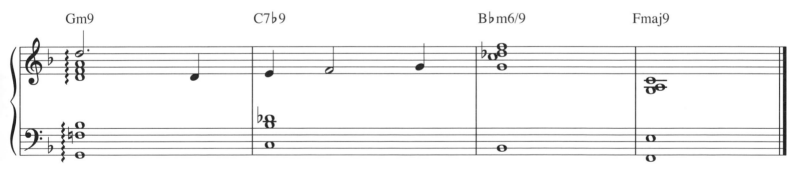

*illustration: dominant without use of the seventh comes from:

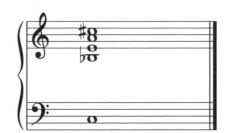

PEOPLE

from FUNNY GIRL

Ballad tempo, flexible, dedicated to Bill Evans.

Words by BOB MERRILL
Music by JULE STYNE

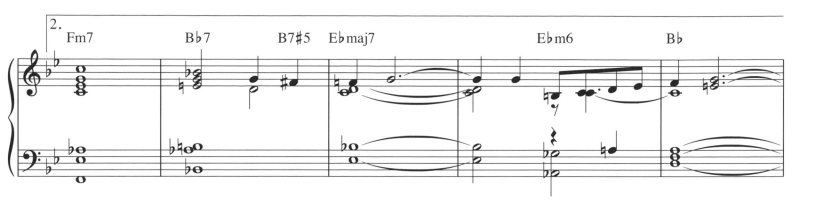

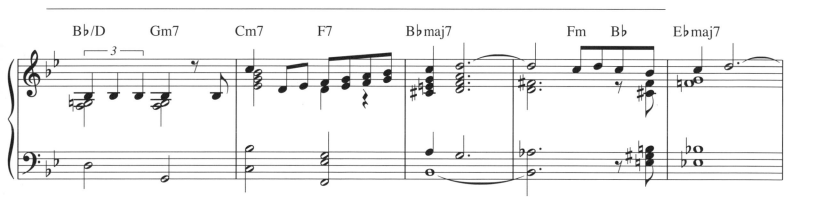

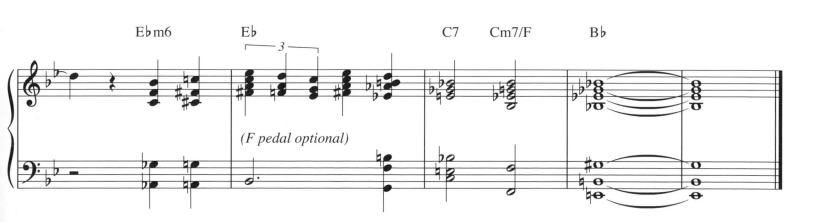

STELLA BY STARLIGHT
from the Paramount Picture THE UNINVITED

A bassline bonanza! Experiment with syncopating
<u>some</u> quarter notes. (advanced)

Words by NED WASHINGTON
Music by VICTOR YOUNG

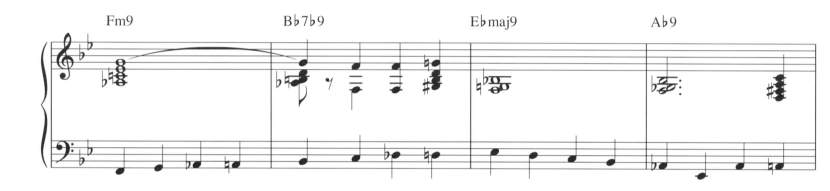

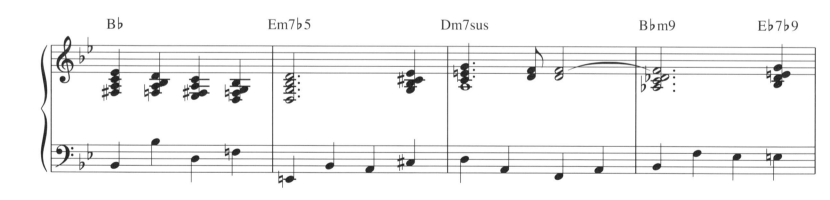

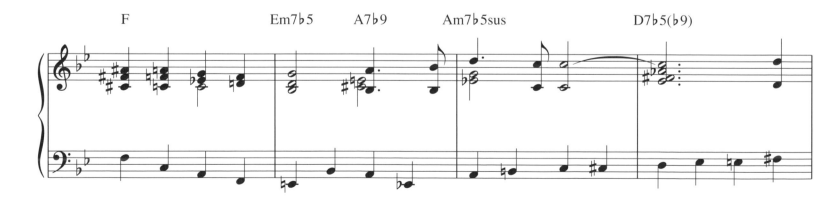

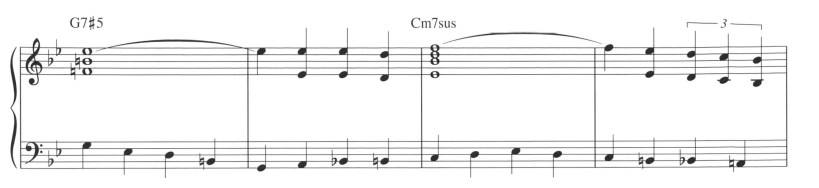

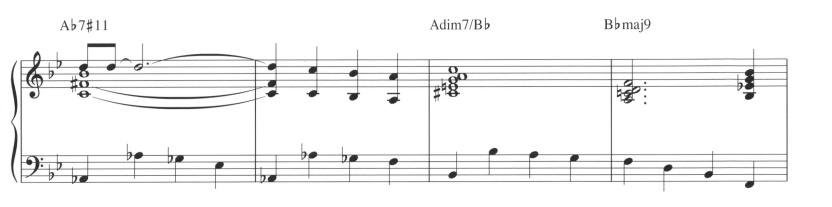

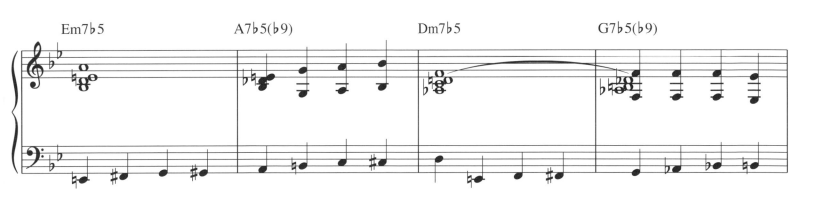

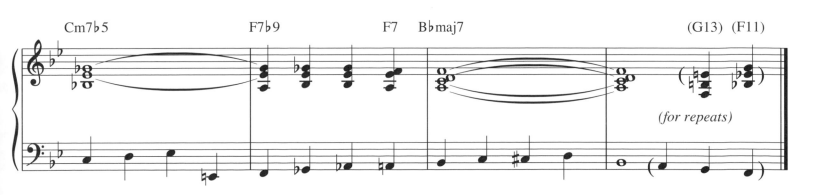

SWEET AND LOVELY

Note the typical Bill Evans device using major seventh and
dominant seventh simultaneously in bars 10 and 12. (advanced)

Words and Music by GUS ARNHEIM,
CHARLES N. DANIELS and HARRY TOBIAS

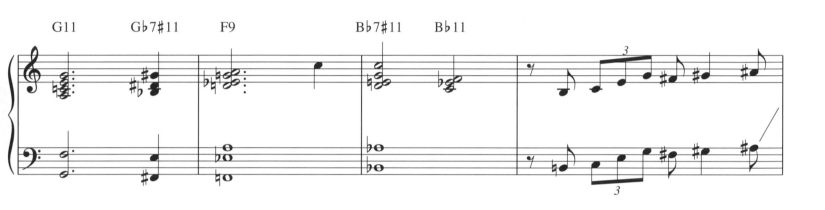

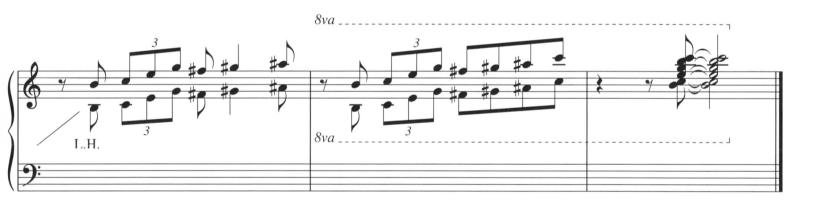

* (alternate bars 3 & 4)

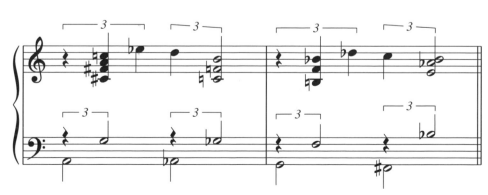

THERE WILL NEVER BE ANOTHER YOU

from the Motion Picture ICELAND

Lyric by MACK GORDON
Music by HARRY WARREN

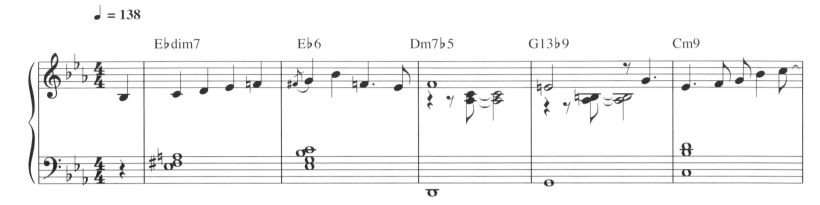

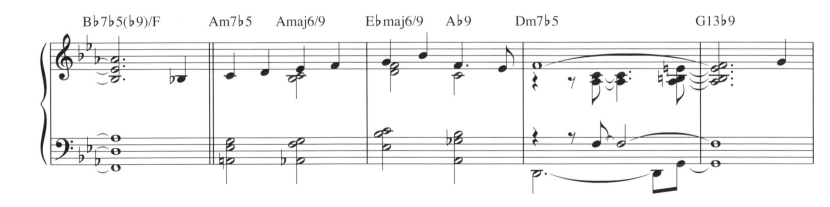

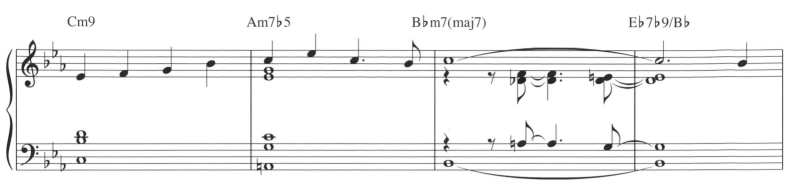

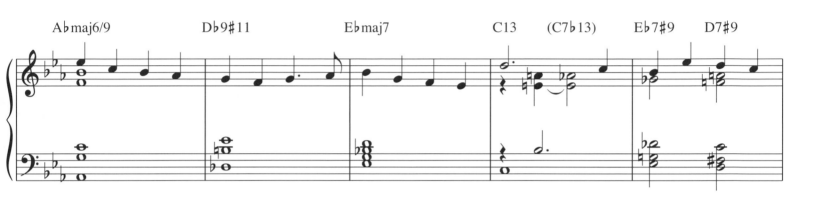

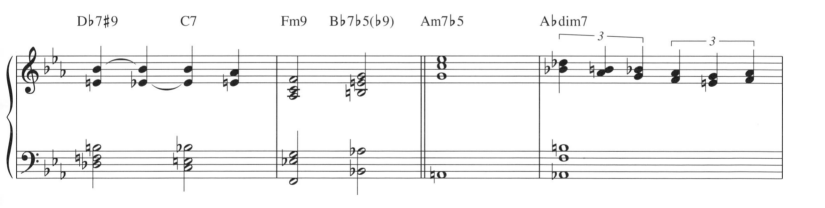

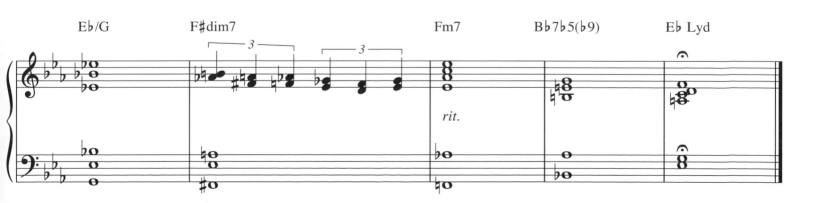

THE TOUCH OF YOUR LIPS

Play up tempo at ♩ = 176, or choose ballad tempo (easy to play).
In the style of Bill Evans.

Words and Music by
RAY NOBLE

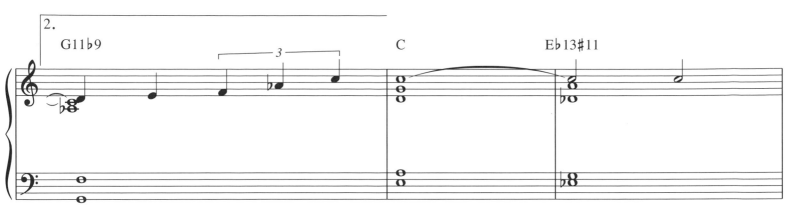

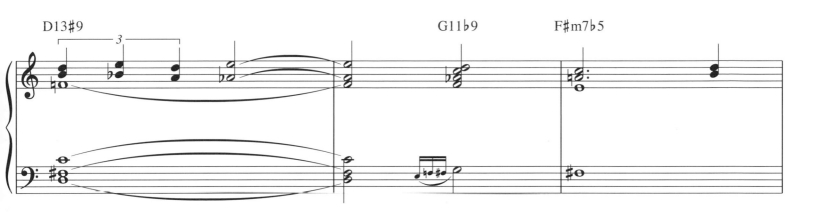

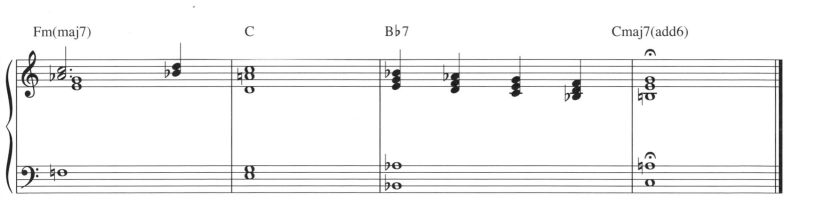

alternate version:

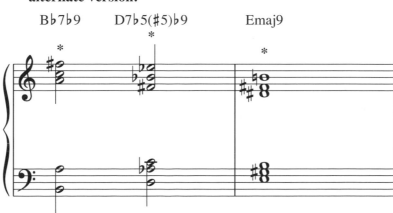

WHAT'S NEW?

Words by JOHNNY BURKE
Music by BOB HAGGART

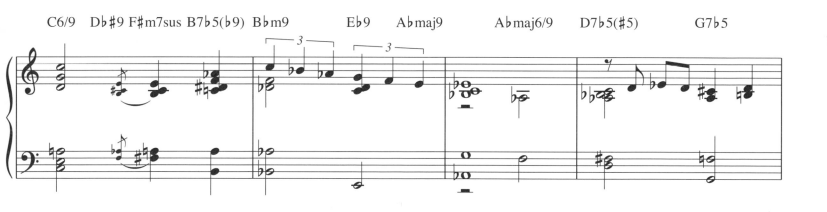

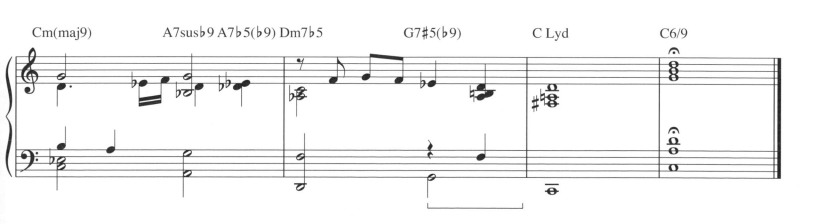

YOU ARE TOO BEAUTIFUL

from HALLELUJAH, I'M A BUM

Words by LORENZ HART
Music by RICHARD RODGERS

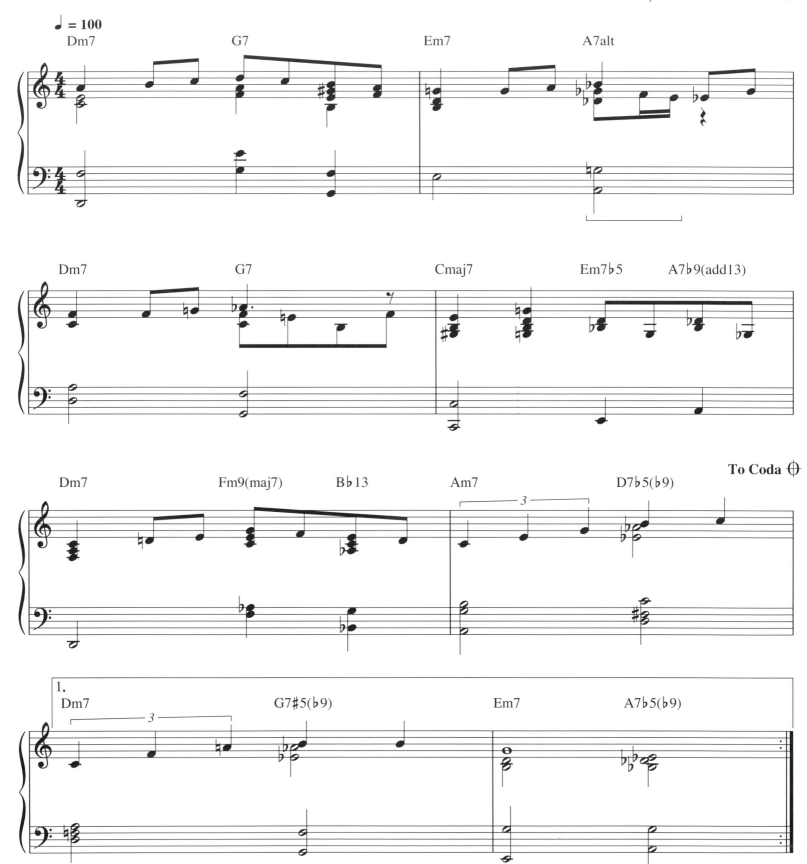

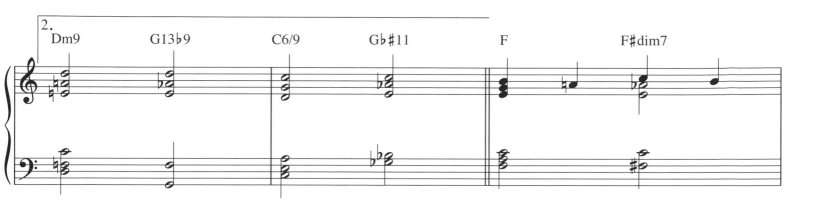

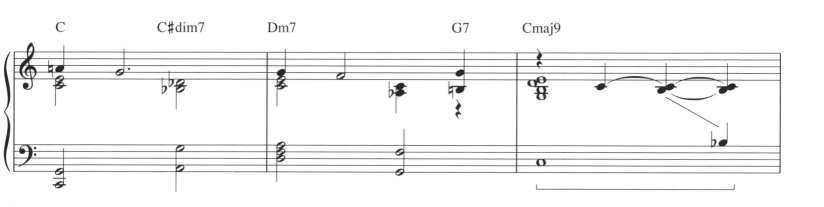

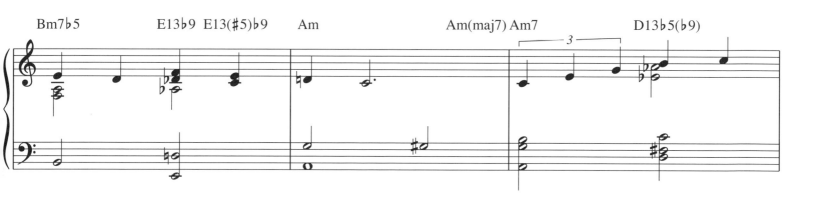

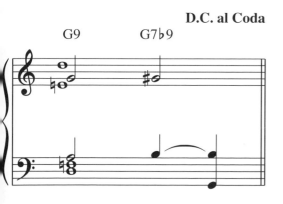

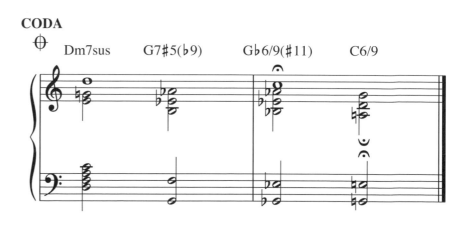

LUSH LIFE

In a Bud Powell ballad mood. (advanced)

Words and Music by
BILLY STRAYHORN

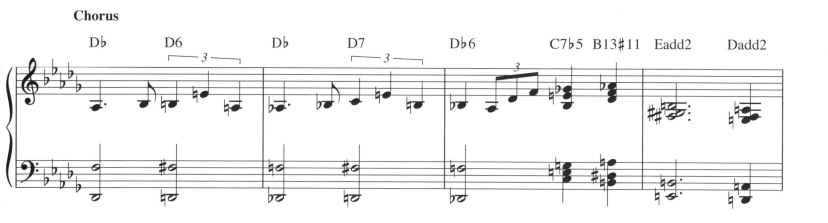

Chorus

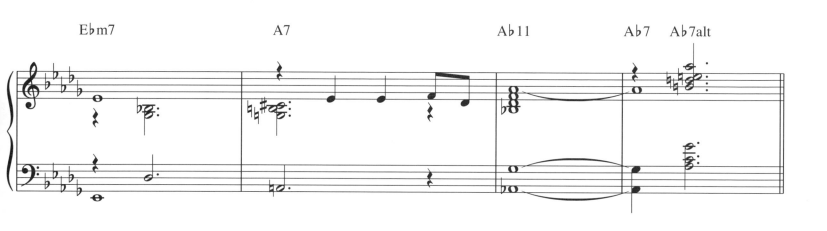

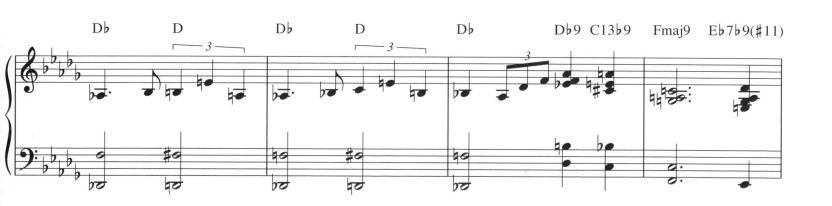

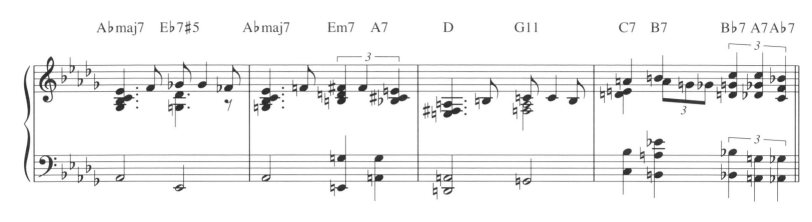

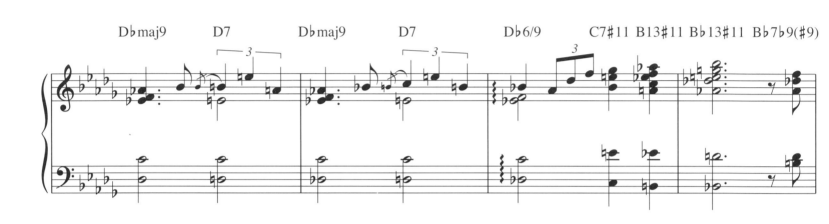

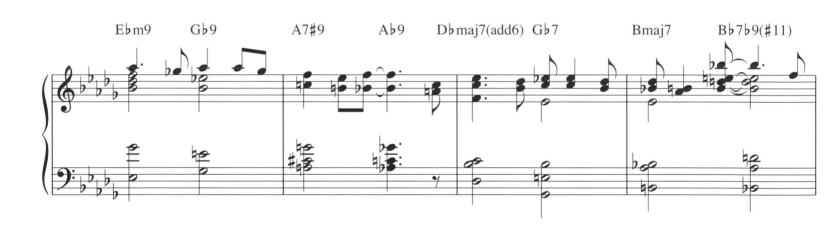